The Eleventh Lost Tribe

Books by LOUIS DANIEL BRODSKY

Poetry

Five Facets of Myself   (1967)* (1995)

The Easy Philosopher   (1967)* (1995)

"A Hard Coming of It" and Other Poems   (1967)* (1995)

The Foul Rag-and-Bone Shop   (1967)* (1969)* (1995)

Points in Time   (1971)* (1995) (1996)

Taking the Back Road Home   (1972)* (1997)

Trip to Tipton and Other Compulsions   (1973)* (1997)

"The Talking Machine" and Other Poems   (1974)* (1997)

Tiffany Shade   (1974)* (1997)

Trilogy: A Birth Cycle   (1974)* (1998)

Cold, Companionable Streams   (1975)*

Monday's Child   (1975)

Preparing for Incarnations   (1975)* (1976)

The Kingdom of Gewgaw   (1976)

Point of Americas II   (1976)

La Preciosa   (1977)

Stranded in the Land of Transients   (1978)

The Uncelebrated Ceremony of Pants Factory Fatso   (1978)

Birds in Passage   (1980)

Résumé of a Scrapegoat   (1980)

Mississippi Vistas: Volume One of *A Mississippi Trilogy*   (1983) (1990)

You Can't Go Back, Exactly   (1988)

The Thorough Earth   (1989)

Four and Twenty Blackbirds Soaring   (1989)

Falling from Heaven: Holocaust Poems of a Jew and a Gentile
   (with William Heyen)   (1991)

Forever, for Now: Poems for a Later Love   (1991)

Mistress Mississippi: Volume Three of *A Mississippi Trilogy*   (1992)

A Gleam in the Eye: Poems for a First Baby   (1992)

Gestapo Crows: Holocaust Poems   (1992)

The Capital Café: Poems of Redneck, U.S.A.   (1993)

Disappearing in Mississippi Latitudes: Volume Two of *A Mississippi
   Trilogy*   (1994)

A Mississippi Trilogy: A Poetic Saga of the South   (1995)*

Paper-Whites for Lady Jane: Poems of a Midlife Love Affair   (1995)

The Complete Poems of Louis Daniel Brodsky: Volume One, 1963–1967
   (edited by Sheri L. Vandermolen)   (1996)

Three Early Books of Poems by Louis Daniel Brodsky, 1967–1969: *The Easy
   Philosopher*, *"A Hard Coming of It" and Other Poems*, and *The Foul Rag-
   and-Bone Shop* *(edited by Sheri L. Vandermolen)*   (1997)

The Eleventh Lost Tribe: Poems of the Holocaust   (1998)

Bibliography (Coedited with Robert Hamblin)

Selections from the William Faulkner Collection of Louis Daniel Brodsky:
A Descriptive Catalogue (1979)

Faulkner: A Comprehensive Guide to the Brodsky Collection
Volume I: The Bibliography (1982)
Volume II: The Letters (1984)
Volume III: *The De Gaulle Story* (1984)
Volume IV: *Battle Cry* (1985)
Volume V: Manuscripts and Documents (1989)

Country Lawyer and Other Stories for the Screen by William Faulkner (1987)

Stallion Road: A Screenplay by William Faulkner (1989)

Biography

William Faulkner, Life Glimpses (1990)

Prose

The Adventures of the Night Riders, Better Known as the Terrible Trio
(with Richard Milsten) (1961)*

Between Grief and Nothing (1964)*

Between the Heron and the Wren (1965)*

Dink Phlager's Alligator *(novella)* (1966)*

The Drift of Things (1966)*

Vineyard's Toys (1967)*

The Bindlestiffs (1968)*

Catchin' the Drift o' the Draft (1997)*

Yellow Bricks (1997)*

* *Unpublished*

The Eleventh Lost Tribe

Poems of the Holocaust

Louis Daniel Brodsky

TIME BEING BOOKS
POETRY IN SIGHT AND SOUND
St. Louis, Missouri

Time Being Books®
10411 Clayton Road
St. Louis, Missouri 63131

Time Being Books® is an imprint of Time Being Press®
St. Louis, Missouri

Time Being Press® is a 501(c)(3) not-for-profit corporation.

Time Being Books® volumes are printed on acid-free paper, and binding
materials are chosen for strength and durability.

ISBN 1-56809-041-2 (Hardcover)
ISBN 1-56809-042-0 (Paperback)

Library of Congress Cataloging-in-Publication Data:

Brodsky, Louis Daniel.
    The eleventh lost tribe : poems of the Holocaust / Louis Daniel
Brodsky. — 1st ed.
        p.   cm.
    ISBN 1-56809-041-2 (hb : alk. paper). — ISBN 1-56809-042-0 (pb : alk.
paper)
    1. Holocaust, Jewish (1939–1945)—Poetry.   I. Title.
PS3552.R623E43   1998
811'.54—dc21   97-49672
                                                                          CIP

Cover art by Edward Boccia, *The Crucifixion*. Courtesy of the artist.
Book design and typesetting by Sheri L. Vandermolen
Manufactured in the United States of America

First Edition, first printing (May 1998)

Acknowledgments

I am indebted to Jerry Call, Editor in Chief of Time Being Books, for collaborating with me in revising these poems. His sure, intuitive sense of what is poetically correct is reassuring.

I also want to thank Sheri L. Vandermolen, Managing Editor of Time Being Books, for her close reading and invaluable revisionary suggestions. She motivates me to reach for my poetic best.

Joe Nicastri read an earlier version of this manuscript and made a number of suggestions.

Three of these poems previously appeared in the following magazines: *Phase and Cycle* ("Victim of the Liberation"); *The Pittsburgh Quarterly* ("Live Hens, April 1940"); *Sepia Poetry Magazine* ("Why Didn't My Father Die in the Fire?").

The following poems, in earlier versions, first appeared in 1993, in a privately printed chapbook titled *Missing in* Aktion: *A Minyan of Survivors*: "The Bitter Riddles of History," "Shower Duty," "Dreamscape with Three Crows," "Struck Dumb," "Teleology," "Listening to a Voice That Never Existed," "Daddies' Girls," "Old Man Rosenblatt: Dresden, London, St. Louis," "Ultimate Sacrifices," "Schlomo Vogelsang: Prague, Auschwitz, St. Louis," "Scarecrow on a Crucifix," "Crow-Magnon Man."

"Teleology" and "Dreamscape with Three Crows" (previously titled "The Crows") appeared in *The Uncelebrated Ceremony of Pants Factory Fatso* (Farmington, Missouri: Farmington Press, 1978).

I consulted *Lodz Ghetto: Inside a Community Under Seige*, compiled and edited by Alan Adelson and Robert Lapides (New York: Penguin Books, 1989), for certain historical facts that I incorporated into the six parts comprised in the poem "Litzmannstadt Ghetto, Lodz, Poland."

For Rachel Ertel,

who demonstrates her compassion for humankind
through the passion of her pursuits
as teacher, scholar, and translator

In the absence of firsthand experience,
Everything we learn
Must necessarily be true
Through secondhand acts, empathy,

But what we trust and believe
By making leaps of imagination
Can only redeem us
In the presence of actual faith.

— Louis Daniel Brodsky, "Epistemology: Teaching the Holocaust to Future Refugees"

Lord, grant us the wisdom
To deduce universal truths from the inscrutable,
Courage to transmute moral confusion to enlightenment,
And compassion to forgive repentant enemies,
Convert them to friends,
That we might dream peace in our sleep,
Choose love over hatred awake,
But never mistake the two for true faith.

— Louis Daniel Brodsky, "Desiderata"

Contents

The Eleventh Lost Tribe

Prologue

According to Plan

The objective, unquestionably,
Will be for them to try,
With their feeble intellection,
To beat Satan and his crew,
Shape a lasting peace out of compassion,
Repudiate and relegate to forgetting's far reaches
Ignorance and bigotry and hatred and cruelty and violence,
Which, otherwise, will shame their potential humanity,
Deny them, in My eyes,
A restored record of love, kindness, and decency,
A heritage commensurate with My intended mercy,
So that women and men,
All the generations of Adam and Eve,
Might venerate My ideal state,
Where war is, at worst, a dead issue,
A mute eunuch's desperate, stillborn outrage,
An undiscoverable source of dementia,
Dementia a schizophrenic coefficient of genocide,
A godless atrocity,
And genocide a dimensionless nonentity outside space and time.
If my latest creations, these new humans,
Will only remember that, being indefensibly dispensable,
They must never resort to Final Solutions,
Rather need to leave the business of immortality to Me
And just trust in My omniscience,
Everything will go, as usual, according to plan.

Litzmannstadt Ghetto

Litzmannstadt Ghetto, Lodz, Poland

For Jerzy Kosinski, 1933–1991

I: Live Hens, April 1940

> *An egg in the ghetto,*
> *God in heaven.*
> — old Yiddish saying

He awakens, this Tuesday morning,
Into a late-April incarnation
Completely disorienting.
Just three days ago, or four,
The celebration of Passover
Reached uneventful culmination,
Achieved a silence so spiritless
That even he, a renegade, *Volksdeutsch* go-between,
Working both inside and out
Of the recently installed Litzmannstadt ghetto,
Couldn't distinguish Jew from Christian,

The fenced-in, dispossessed Semites
From unstigmatized Germans and Poles
Boasting no "Jewish yellow" on their clothes,
Neither bands just below the shoulders
Nor Stars of David on their right breasts.
An Aryan himself, Polish by birth,
Jude by oblique heritage
Resulting from intermarriages centuries deep,
He passes the blackened, stony remains
Of the gutted Old Town Synagogue on Wolborska Street
As he weaves toward his rendezvous

Near Baluter Ring station
With one of Chaim Rumkowski's "strong arms,"
A policeman of the people,
Feared for his merciless treatment of violators,
A vindictive stickler for codes
Tyrannically imposed on the enclosed victims
Out of his own misguided desire
To comply with the Eldest of the Jews' wishes
To save his "beloved citizens"
From whatever sinister disposition
Even his graphic imagination can't yet conjecture.

He carries in the inner folds of his trench coat
Three live hens,
Which he'll sell to his contact for fifteen marks apiece,
Who will profit handsomely
By quadrupling that price to those still flush
After their "planned resettlement," begun last November,
To this contagion-infested ghetto
For pernicious, gentile-bloodletting Jew-vermin,
Gypsies, atheists, and agnostic misfits,
Still naively euphoric over the prospect
Of having a fresh egg to eat, a precious egg,

Who, too soon, will realize that even an egg
And the savory white and dark meat
They'll finally carve and eat
One ephemeral Feast of Lights night
Can't possibly compete with starvation
Or even begin to meet their daily nutritional needs
To keep up productivity at the makeshift shops,
Where they sweat to supply uniforms, shoes,
Bullet casings, mattresses, boxes, bags,
And stationery for the Wehrmacht, NSDAP,
Elite Death's Head SS unit of the dread Gestapo,

Sweating in the desperate belief that their efforts,
Respected for quality of craftsmanship,
Their inventiveness and meticulousness
Despite subhuman working conditions,
All in exchange for food and fuel,
Will merit them commutation of a future
Whose details neither they nor their subjugators
Have yet fully finalized
At the mind's still-undreamed,
-Unconvened Wannsee Conference of Doomed Humans,
Since both, at this juncture,

Although neither knows it,
Have gratuitously deluded themselves into thinking
All will end well
Because all *is* well with their notions of truth,
Righteousness, salvation, redemption,
*

Well with God's ordained final solution
That someone, if not He,
Must institute the necessary sacrifices
To ensure the fulfillment of His covenant,
Both "races" convinced of their ultimate superiority,
Their "chosen" state of grace.

And so he ruminates on this late-April day
As he nears the fence where his Jew partner, Rosenswieg,
For forty-five marks,
Will buy his three hens
And parlay them openly on the street,
In the still-giddy black market,
Into quarter-chicken plates fifteen marks each,
Eggs at two and a half marks each.
But as he turns the corner of Zielony Rynek Street,
He sees armed guards swarming about a man on the ground,
Whom they're viciously beating with truncheons, kicking.

Approaching with growing trepidation,
He suddenly recognizes the unfortunate as his contact.
Wheeling on the balls of his feet,
He takes off running, at full tilt,
Back in the direction from which he's just come.
But the fowls inside his coat break loose
And scatter under his feet in a shattering clatter
That distracts those gathered around the set-upon Rosenswieg,
Not fifty meters away at the border.
He trips over the hysterically scurrying birds and falls,
But not before a *Volksdeutsch*,

One of his own Polish-German kind,
Patrolling the fence enclosing the ghetto,
Takes hasty aim with his government-issue Mauser
And unloads a fusillade of bullets
Into his chest and neck and head.
In a single motion, this same nameless guard,
Who, until now, has overlooked their daily dissimulation,
Reloads his clip, opens and closes his bolt,
And fires into the crowd of Jews on the other side,
Indiscriminately picking off
One, two, three, four, five live hens.

II: Temporary Solutions, September 1941

Something doesn't want this ghetto decimated.
No matter what typhus, dysentery,
And their equally virulent co-evil, starvation,
Do to de-Jew this misbegotten populace,
It seems to survive and multiply.
What a cruel, black-humorous joke
Someone in the universe keeps playing,
Casting us into this Litzmannstadt prison,
Feeding us dishwater soup once a day from communal kitchens,
Allotting us a daily ration of meager grams of bread,
Fewer yet of rotten potatoes.

And now, five months after celebrating Passover,
Our second in this scrofulous quarter,
We're visited with a plague of fifty thousand refugees
From Prague, Berlin, Vienna, and Cologne;
We, with not enough matzo
To properly admonish our most recent Pharaoh/
Nebuchadnezzar/Hadrian/Savonarola;
We, quarantined to this pestiferous dance-of-death pit,
Doing everything possible
To achieve a zero-population condition,
Only to be increased, glutted, by additional walking cadavers.

In this dreary September, when coal and wood
Are scarcer than hens' teeth
(And hens haven't been seen in Baluty for a year),
We draw naturally closer,
Eight, ten to a room, not to stay warm
So much as resist having our families separated.
Some of us, those who have physical strength,
Still hold to beliefs that eventually the wall will fall,
Roosevelt will declare war,
And we'll be liberated, delivered to our former callings
All across Europe . . . some are still filled with hope,

Though most know this mission is no Crusade
But rather the strangest journey
Moses' children have ever made into the wilderness.
*

This morning, heading toward the tailor shop on Wolborska,
I see my name on Rumkowski's latest public notice,
Consigning me to deportation and forced labor in Berlin,
Me and a thousand other fortunate conscriptees,
Who are at least going to a known destination
And won't die from eating the air that feeds us
Or the mud that buries us deeper and deeper,
Year after year, millenniums on end.

III: Birthday Celebration, April 1942

As I move inexorably toward fifty,
It seems this Polish ghetto,
Where I've survived these past two years,
Deepens with each passing day, widens.
Now it's impossible to distinguish faces,
Remember names of my oldest friends;
Even my parents have assumed an opacity,
A cast to their skin cadaverous for its pallor,
A sepulchral clue to the inscrutable future,
Into which, too soon, they'll disappear.
All life's signs of dissolution whisper in my ear,

But I can't discern their message for my hunger;
My spirit's starvation is a predatory,
Insatiably voracious dragon
Striking with gratuitous vengeance.
Even in my dreams I hear it hissing,
Clawing through my bowels like peristalsis,
A giant lizard
Hiding in the cavities of my Jew-rassic skeleton.
My eyes are singed by its fiery breathing.
Everything within my vision is tinged crimson.
Flesh melts to a translucent husk over the bones.

I can't even fathom
How I've managed to last this long,
Feeding on fetid "nothing soup" once a day,
A ten-decagram loaf of bread weekly,
Coffee-water twice daily,
Learning to do without my children
And the amenities that made living wholesome
And filled, with silver and gold threads,
Empty spaces in the moral fabric,
Holes that naturally tatter
In the process of atomistic decay and scattering.

Lately, I've been having extended lapses,
Diaspora hallucinations, perhaps,
In which I imagine my robed soul
*

Enthroned beneath the dome
Of a nondenominational house of worship,
Reciting non-*Kiddush* over the most delicious nonwine
My lips have ever sipped,
Nibbling nonmatzos made of kosher nonoats,
Reciting non-Psalms praising non-God,
Saying non-*Kaddish* for nonvictims like my non-self,
Seeking nonmiracles to let us die anon.

IV: No Choices for the "Chosen," June 1942

Each day the deportations —
Regular as Sunday Mass to a devout Catholic,
Sabbath to a practicing Jew.
And now the food supply has run dry;
Even a rotten turnip or beet
Is considered a delicacy, not to be had
For any zlotys, reichsmarks, or "Rumkies."
Ration coupons sneer at us.
We eat the putrid air in this Baluty cesspool,
Sip soup, clear as our urine, when it's there.
Oh, for a taste of potato, a bite of sausage!

"Give us this day our daily bread" echoes in our heads
Like a fold's desperate plea to its shepherd;
In this Jewish ghetto,
The Lord's Prayer is a snare of maggots.
Those of us still lucky enough
To stumble to our places of work,
Perform despite aching gums, ubiquitous lice,
And continuous groaning of the stomach,
Do so to elude Rumkowski's transportation list.
A few yet believe productivity will feed us,
Free us from this sadistic dream,

But most of us know deep down
That hope is beyond all hope
And that, ultimately, no one will escape
The liquidation of this living Valley of the Dead.
However, what none of us has fathomed,
Dared imagine or conjecture past the obvious,
Is neither *why* nor *when* we're going
So much as *what* lies ahead,
What apocalyptic desecration
Might possibly make us wish we could still choose
Between starvation, freezing, and terminal disease.

V: Mass Evacuation, September 1–12, 1942

Why, after all these years, decades,
Is sleep such a reeking cesspool?
Just because I pulled a sanitation wagon
Past Baluter Ring station twice daily
Is no reason these grotesque visions should persist
Interminably, interminably. Or is it?
Is there no eluding these nightmarish chimeras?
It's months shy of half a century
Since that mass evacuation began,
And yet the panic of that first day of September
Is as familiar today as the back of my hand,

As graphic as the misaligned blue numerals
Tattooed above my left wrist,
That day the vans arrived at our hospitals
On Lagiewnicka, Wesola, and Drewnowska streets
And routed out all their patients,
The insane as well as those suffering typhus,
Dysentery, and decrepitude.
So unannounced, so matter-of-fact that *Aktion*,
That prelude to the deportation of twenty thousand of us,
Those of us over sixty-five, those of us under ten,
Herded into trucks and wagons,

Taken to freight transports, cattle cars,
To be scattered to whatever fate we couldn't conceive
As possibly being even more inhumane than starvation,
Freezing, hanging, disease, the firing squad —
Oh, death by any other name much sweeter!
All week, truck brakes screeching to a halt,
First before the old-age home on Dworska Street,
Then along Rybna, then to the tenements,
Our own Jewish police, *Ordnungsdienstes*,
Shouting *"Alle Juden raus!"*
Followed by the Germans themselves,

Banging their rifle butts against our doors,
Dragging out our precious babies, our enfeebled;
And always, in the distance, gunshots,
*

Dogs barking, screams, mothers moaning,
Uselessly refusing to let go of their parents and children.
The dread of that scourge! And for what?
To achieve *Judenrein*?
Evacuation, resettlement, deportation —
Macabre euphemisms, synonyms for genocide.
Even now, every night, my dreams still stink
Of the dreck we collected from pots,

Loaded in our wagon, and dumped just beyond the fence
And of the pervasive stench of cadavers,
Everywhere decomposing:
Yellow, purple, black, with pus-oozing scabs,
Corpses emaciated or swollen, naked,
Limp or stiff, defiled by fat, bile-green flies.
How ironic that all seems to me now,
The naiveté of us who accidentally outlasted that riot,
Trying to justify war, hunger, torture,
First and last causes,
God's inscrutable ways, believing we'd survived

Because we'd been able to accommodate to primitive conditions
Or because, as the "chosen,"
We'd been delivered by the spirit of Moses
To protect and perpetuate eternally
What is great and right and hereafter.
How ironic those two notices were
That Biebow issued after twelve nightmarish days,
Demanding resumption of "normal" work on the fourteenth
To coincide with the start of Rosh Hashanah.
How ironic to be fetching rations again next morning,
Wishing each other well for the new year.

VI: "Liberation," January 19, 1945

To have endured, since early '40,
Through such continuously deteriorating metamorphoses,
Only to end up in this malfunctional septic tank
In the basement of the paper-products factory
At 36 Lagiewnicka Street,
Where he, a civil engineer with advanced degrees
From Berlin and Heidelberg universities,
Has hidden from Biebow and his barbaric Kripo
These past three days,
Is beyond his rational capacity to describe —
Hunger is far more articulate; death is Shakespeare.

Here he sits amidst his own shit,
Shivering in this twenty-foot-deep pit
(The frigid outdoors would seem like summer breezes),
One dim light bulb laboring to outwit its own physics,
Oxygen asphyxiating itself by the minute,
Forming a vacuum in this temporary abyss,
Where this victim of his own inevictable desire to survive
Yet exists in ten inches of constantly dripping feces
Seeping through cracks in his makeshift hideout,
Trying to stave off typhus, vanquish dysentery,
Elude doomsday's grisly execution.

Were he to calculate his speculations,
He might approximate that fewer than a thousand people,
Actually 888,
Of a population indigenous or otherwise relocated to Lodz,
Relegated to its Litzmannstadt ghetto,
Which, at its height, caged 300,000 human hearts,
Twice that many ears and eyes,
Quadruple that number of arms and legs,
And God only knows how many aborted dreams,
Are alive at this late hour,
Cowering in concealments as vile as this crypt of his.

Furthermore, he'd be astounded by the Nazi deracination
Of European Jewry,
Singled out for its ethnic success
*

To be sacrificed to a ranting madman's fantasies
Of creating and leaving behind,
For posterity to admire, emulate, and perpetuate,
A Third Reich so undefiled,
So totally God-like in its *Übermensch*-tality,
No children born to the planet Earth
Would ever fail to pay obeisance
To Germany's *Herrenvolk*.

But today, for reasons stranger than intuition,
He senses a diminishing intensity of silence.
Previously, on brief forays
To locate bread, potatoes, drinking water,
He's noticed nine mass graves,
Each able to accommodate a hundred emaciated bodies,
Dug by less fortunate compatriots
Before they were transported from Radogoszcz station
To destinations he'd learn to call Chelmno and Auschwitz.
This morning, though he doesn't yet know it,
He'll hear in Russian the word for "liberation,"

Be told he can come up out of his shit hole,
Walk through the gate at Baluter Ring station,
And, if he chooses, keep going
As far as his imagination might limp
Or his indomitable corpse progress him
Before his destiny expires
Fifty years from this epiphany in the life of mankind.
Though dazed, he'll not fail to notice those open graves
Containing shadows of the 888 souls
Who never made that final journey to the Lodz cemetery,
And he'll wave to his other self as he goes by.

Survivors of the Death Camps

Rosh Hashanah for a Survivor

Auschwitz-sounds resound in his throbbing head
This crisp, September-ending a.m.,
Resonate like a V-18 radial engine
Cranking a Corsair's four-bladed prop
To shrill overwinding
Or Allied rockets and bombs dropping over Dresden.
He winces from pain strafing his indefensible brain.
Suddenly, the blades change pitch;
Those reports metamorphose into horrific moaning;
The living dead, slowly, pitifully dying,
Fill his daymares, this judgment day,
With cries of leniency for their tormentors.

Baffled by his psyche's plea for compassion and decency,
Despite fate's eagerness to wreak reprisal,
No matter how inadequate,
Revenge for those timeless Reich-crimes,
He prays to whatever wayward messianic spirit may prevail
That YHWH make Himself available,
Disclose His requirements for collective atonement.
This meek man knows that, tonight,
When the shofar blows, he'll break a loaf of challah,
Spread an apple with honey,
Get drunk, and weep for unredeemed sinners,
Not for his own lonely soul.

Shower Duty

For Ruth and Dick Vaughan

This forlorn Wednesday morning,
He focuses as best he can on prerecorded music
Wafting down through speakers
Recessed in the ceiling of the Kaffee Haus,
Where he breakfasts daily.
This morning, as he tries to listen,
The notes transform into almond-scented waves
Vibrating his ears, nostrils, and brain,
Which, strangely, retains its capacity from the old days
For translating moans, groans, choking bellows
From Zyklon B vapors spraying through showers and vents
In a concentration camp, Auschwitz,
Death's Canaan,
He yet labors in nightly, five decades later,

Though he died then,
Asphyxia of the spirit the cause of his crystallization,
That insidious disease he contracted over three years
While "assisting" countless numbered victims
(Political enemies of the state, Christ-killers,
Sexual deviants, the mentally and physically ill),
Bareboned, shivering, arms raised,
Squeezed, like cigarettes in a pack,
Into quickly constructed "disinfection facilities"
His superiors also assigned him to "tidy up"
After each use — hose, through drains,
Blood, mucus, urine, vomit, shit,
Tears, memories, too-long-endured fear,
Hebrew and Yiddish prayers shimmering in the mist.

This forlorn morning, sipping coffee,
He gags on strains of Wagner's operas —
Das Rheingold, Die Walküre, Götterdämmerung —
Infiltrating his fragile vessel.
Next, he recognizes excerpts from overtures
To *Tannhäuser* and *Lohengrin*,
Recoils, and grows rigid in his constricted booth.
Everyone in the café seems to be shedding clothes,
Getting ready to parade naked to another location;
*

Only he knows their fate.
Abruptly, he stands up and shouts, "Wait! Wait!
Don't go in there — *verboten! Verboten!*"
Embarrassed for him, they cringe
As he rushes out to catch a breath of air.

Dreamscape with Three Crows

Three crows,
Like gargoyles poised on a cathedral's lip,
Cluster at highway's edge,
Heedless of his passing
For the rabbit their beaks and talons obliterate.
Unnerved, he conjures an unholy image,
In which the repugnant birds are a trinity of Black Shirts
From a late-'30s propaganda poster
Caricaturing him as a Christ-killer
They're bludgeoning bloody with their scepters.

Pain chews through his forehead;
He squints, loses visual acuity.
His eyes confuse their main guide,
The highway's centerline, with railroad track —
Eerily, nightmarish cattle cars
Rumble hysterically through his ears' tunnel.
Mirrors inside his mind shatter
As though pecked by crows escaped from a cage
Hung from his brain's cranial rafters
By a Piranesian chain.

Suddenly, flapping shadows,
Like wings attached to blunt, black bodies,
Penetrate his retinas.
Scorched flesh, singed feathers,
Crackling fat, ashes permeate his senses,
As if something in his attic has recently died.
He hesitates going upstairs,
Into his psyche's jagged garret,
Where terror still breathes acrid Auschwitz air,
For fear that corpses might be stacked there.

Schreiber, Bard of Belzec

I: Struck Dumb

For a poet who knows only loneliness,
Even recent holocausts
Are just dust-thoughts caught on gauzy breezes
Fanned by acrid memories,
Stations along a crisscrossing railway
Running through a landfill of Bosch-monsters,
Windmills doleful Quixotes tilt at with their souls.

Whether it be dissolution of vows or bones
By fire, state decree, rabbi, or Pope
Is inconsequential to him.
He composes lines one filament at a time,
Like a spider, bird, bee, death,
Building his own web, nest, hive, sepulcher
To protect himself against the elements.

Rarely does he surface from work
To survey the terrain,
Made up of mass graves covered with erika,
Clover, dandelions, ivy;
He knows too well who goes there
And what ancient languages
Their inarticulate moans evoke,

Even though, these days,
He doesn't linger above ground
Or mingle with those placing sprays,
Lighting Yahrzeit candles.
Long ago, he transcended despair,
Seeking safety in imagination's sanctuary,
Where the air floated no ash-motes

Or odors of incinerated flesh.
Only there, he discovered,
Could he rid himself of doubt,
Exist in solitude exempt from cruelty,
And perpetuate illusory metaphors
By shaping images of peace, gentleness, and love
From greed, racism, obscene deeds.

But for this privileged immunity
From committing "crimes against humanity,"
He's paid a steep price.
After translating God's silence into verse,
He always recites it to a world
Unable to read his quivering lips.
He's spoken to no one in seven years.

II: Kapo Poet

No matter how assiduously
He strives to invite laughter into his life,
Erase firestorms from the sky
With rainbows from the sun's prism,
Pursue love and work with virtuous fervor,
Never losing sight of deus-ex-machina options,
Christian or Judaic immaterial to his poetic intellect,
Provided he maintains his faithful obeisance
To a belief in one God and a Messiah to come,
He can't seem to repudiate
Or even elude the mortifying suspicion
That sanity has taken permanent leave of his senses,
Bequeathed him the shadows of inchoate madness,
Not meanspiritedness
But the spirit's black-hole collapse,
Whose undertow will suck his soul out of orbit,
Direct its predestined trajectory into frigid emptiness.

This rainy, postwar morning in early June,
His eyes are innocent bystanders
To the atrocities his mind commands his right hand to commit
As its fingers and wrist muscles
Contract stiffly under orders from Below,
Pleading *nolo contendere*, *Befehl ist Befehl*,
Even as the pen thrashes like a whip
Across the blue lines comprised in the doomsday book
He's been assigned to keep balanced day to day,
Accounting for those who've paid their dues
By placing a crucifix beside their names,
Those who've fallen gravely into debt
With tattoo-numerals forming crude Stars of David —
Poems of a sadomasochistic Kapo,
Poems over which the only control he exercises
Is their very execution,
Each his own death certificate.

III: No Refuge for a Refugee Poet

Strange how he can be on vacation six days,
Away, not only physically but emotionally,
From his all-consuming survivor's routine
Of trying to stay two steps ahead of the curse,
Whose demons have been programmed
To decode the metaphors and symbols
Imagination dictates to his creative intellect
Relating him to his hiding place
And it to ghetto-ridden America,
Policed by Christian ghosts,
Who themselves never succeeded at making peace
With their Protestant Lord God of hosts,
At least in this melting pot,
Where his emaciated spirit landed
After Allied soldiers bailed him out
Of civilization's Jews' debtors' prison.

Strange how six days lying low
In an oceanside bungalow
At a Florida resort lush with palm trees,
Sleeping for hours at a time on a chaise longue
Beneath a nurturing sun,
Languishing wine-drunk afternoons and evenings
Wasn't enough indolence
To enable him to elude those old fe-fi-fo doldrums:
Stoking the ovens with Jew-bones like his own,
Shoveling their ashes into carts,
Over and over.
Now, deported home to his destiny's death camp,
He finds his mind's blunt-tipped pick
Once again attempting to chisel unbroken lines
From his memory's craggy pits,
Poetry's Belzec.

IV: Teleology

Mobile homes and sparsely settled farmhouses
Share the desolate, snow-speckled land
With sleeping sows,
Empty fields, barns, huddled cows,
And feckless hours and seconds
That pass single file like a cortège.
The bareboned trees are naked prisoners
Standing in line behind a winter door
Leading to the lethal showers,
Where ghosts disappear into ashen air
Like gas through chimney stacks.

Curious, that in this baleful daytime Sheol,
His mind would have him invent a quiescent God
Who manifests His will
By convincing him to accept as merciful
These specters of doom that infiltrate his brain,
Without so much as begging for an explanation,
Let alone questioning His motives.
In truth, he refuses to acknowledge a season so dreary,
So brooding,
Void of birth, rife with death,
As an occurrence worthy of His purposive covenant.

Despite Belzec, he can't believe
God's continuity isn't infinitely positive
Or his own isn't finite, incomplete, ephemeral.
On the other hand,
What he's construed today, he confesses,
Might just be philosophical speculation,
Suppressed death wish, mind-mirage,
His homeless soul searching for some earthly design,
Groping to locate a warm corner
In a formless, frigid universe
By making itself heard in desperate survival-verse.

V: Listening to a Voice That Never Existed

He sits in the recording studio with his engineer,
Listening to his own lips and tongue
Reciting words, lines, and stanzas
His imagination built into poetic fortresses
Over four decades ago,
During those initial postwar years in America,
When his spirit spent extended hiatuses
Soaring through memory's wilderness,
Translating God's silence from that plangent event.

Now, editing verses he's just finished taping,
He can't identify his voice as his own,
As though the speaker, naming camps and tortures
From A to Z — Auschwitz to Zyklon B —
Were chanting echoes of an even older specter,
A victim he barely escaped becoming
For having been liberated
(The rest of his family not as fortunate)
Physically intact, with one horrid exception.

Maybe he's hard of hearing;
Perhaps his lack of recognition
Yet derives from suppressing the fact that he,
Prewar Poland's foremost poet,
Who survived Belzec, headed for America,
And arrived numb and dumb
For the first seven years of his new life,
Has never really spoken these poems before today . . .
A dead man wrote them.

Battenberg Lace

Hoping to erase creases
Disking his forehead, furrowing both cheeks,
Branching past his beaked nose
Like fidgeting mythic tributaries
Dripping down Mississippi and Euphrates deltas
Or moating medieval fortifications,
He obsessively rubs a paper napkin over his face
(Fleetingly, he recalls once making grave rubbings
In a remote cloister of Westminster Abbey).

Grease collects on its white expanse
Like coal-dust smudges
Or blurred fingerprints on a police report.
He studies these vaguely telltale shapes,
Rorschach splotches,
As if fathoming creatures coursing in turbid shallows
Of a river surging upstream through memory
Or focusing twitching protozoans
Under maximum magnification.

But no matter how vigorously he repeats this motion,
Grease keeps reappearing;
The tributaries won't stop gushing.
He senses his fluids leaking
As though, like an open bag of chocolate morsels
Set too near a baker's oven, he were melting, melting,
Flowing instead like smelters' molten lead.
Suddenly, he swims amidst the darting creatures
Fluting through memory's headwaters toward extinction.

Soon, bones and flesh will evaporate in the stratosphere
Above Chelmno's belching crematory stacks,
As once they almost did — his bones, his flesh —
Leaving an indelible stain
On God's freshly cleaned and pressed
Battenberg-lace sky.

Moses Reich

This sunny June a.m., dazed to the world,
He awakens and drives five miles in the dark,
Parks at an all-too-familiar motel he once called home
(Lately, he's taken up residence
Inside a rusted bin at a recycling center),
And debates whether or not he should enter for breakfast.
After all, he dresses au naturel these days
(Regression has been his most bracing discovery in ages).
Yet on the other end of the dialectical spectrum
Is the technical phenomenon he's at a loss to explain:
Even if he were fully clothed,
An eerie nimbus would hide his private identity
From eyes intent on disrobing him in public
For the sake of exposing scabs, tattoos, lacerations,
Black-and-blue bruises, Teutonic numerals
Circumscribing and asphyxiating his survivor's psyche
(Souvenirs of his years as a postgraduate student
At the University of Auschwitz-Birkenau,
Where he majored in gratuitous brutality and victimization —
He had the best professors Western culture had ever germinated —
And even wrote a published dissertation,
*The Effects of Employing Zyklon B as an Efficacious Remedy
For the Systematic Extermination of Persistent Rodents
And Other Noxious Vermin*).

But he's starving,
Hasn't eaten a morsel in days, weeks, half a century,
Since his liberation from Buchenwald,
His arrival on America's shores,
His move to St. Louis to live in a youth hostel
Sponsored by the Cheshed Shel Emeth Society
And assume a job in a doctor's office
(He received his advanced degree
From the Medical College of Berlin),
Administering shots, operating the x-ray machine,
Doing odd jobs in exchange for room and board,
Studying nights to pass his exams,
Become fully licensed,
Finally securing a permanent position
As a registered pharmacist at a drugstore in Ladue,
*

Where, until a few weeks ago
Or forty years, possibly,
He earned his solitary livelihood dispensing prescriptions
To affluent hypochondriacs and the truly ill . . .
Until his obituary appeared in the *Post-Dispatch*,
To the notice of an exceptionally select group of customers,
Who had, after a long stretch of meager communication,
Come to address him as Moses
(He never broke his habit
Of calling them "sir" and "ma'am") . . .

Until now, when hunger's overtaken his soul,
Forced him to return to this motel today,
Where he lived by himself for more than twenty years,
This ghetto not altogether unlike those he knew "at home,"
In order to break the fast he's been keeping
Since deportation eternities back,
Slake his starvation,
That emptiness his eviscerated spirit can never fill,
Never satisfy no matter how much food
He might shovel in to help him forget his bone-thin appearance,
That skeletal self the patrons in this dining room
Would exploit once again
Just for the thrill of reminding themselves
That certain subspecies will always be *Untermenschen*,
Whether killed or permitted to exist,
While others will always rise to the surface as superior,
Those chosen by God
To guide the Aryan race out of the desert,
Into Valhalla's oasal milk and honey . . .
Until this sunny June a.m.,
When even death can't deny Moses Reich his right to die.

Victim of the Liberation

This gray, rainy a.m.
Is a beggar's baggy, tattered greatcoat,
Within whose convoluted folds he gropes,
An altogether insignificant insect
Scrabbling to keep from forfeiting its husk,
Stranded completely out in the open,
Exposed to cruel gratuitousness
In the middle of a floating island,
Earthly atoll in a universal ocean,
Neither Laputa nor Blefuscu,
Rather Gregor Samsa's floor — a spectral nexus.

Ah, there's the resonating correspondence!
This gray beggar's morning is Prague, Majdanek.
He kneels at Kafka's feet,
Poised to accept cyanide wafers,
A fascist sacrament that scratches the throat,
Burns the bowels, innocently received
As his beetle feet spur his imagination,
Hoping to overturn the jury's verdict,
Locate a way out of this loboto-maze,
Walk upright, naked, beneath the acid rain
Without having it descend as Zyklon B vapors.

The Last of a Dying Breed

He awakens naked from a dead sleep,
Assumes a sedentary position on the edge of his bed
That approximates a compromise
Between an ape resting on its haunches,
Contemplating its own vegetative numbness,
And the pose of Rodin's *Thinker*,
In all its introspective suggestiveness.
A throbbing erection, lodged at the focal point
Where his emotions' Tigris and Euphrates join
And flow into the greater body of his brain's ocean,
Pains him into consciousness.
He ejaculates; heated semen from his screaming scrotum
Explodes all over his stomach,
Sullies the sheets that have shrouded him in slumber.
Each morning for a lifetime of sublimated pleasure,
He's performed this onanistic ritual
As if to relieve himself of the need to achieve climax
With creatures other than succubi he fantasizes nightly,
Who seep over from dreams into reality,
Accompany him through his daily routine
Of teaching refugees how to identify their death wishes,
Discriminate between suicide and euthanasia,
Distinguish friend from enemy,
Keep quiet despite enduring the most vicious atrocities.
After all, he hasn't remained abstemious all these years
Just to set the right example,
Refrained from casual delights
Simply out of respect for his brutally defiled wife,
Who, unlike him, died at Treblinka,
Or to prove that suffering can redeem the living,
If not the victims of holocausts.
Indeed, quite the contrary;
If he could get an erection with a woman,
Slut or lover,
He would savor the ecstasy of flesh connecting with flesh,
Know again the intimacy he shared with Miriam,
That beautiful Jewish lady wrested from him,
Barely three weeks into their marriage,
Back in Lublin, in the summer of '43.
Ah, but for half a century,
*

He's practiced psychotherapy
In St. Louis's flourishing Jewish community,
Handling death, divorce, child abuse, eating disorders,
Chemical dependency, and sexual dysfunction,
A successful but enigmatic recluse, inscrutable,
A credit to his people, his religion
For his impeccable international reputation,
Yet always, in the repressed depths of his silent psyche,
A masturbator — the last of his family line.

A Terminal Survivor

Another hapless Saturday
Trapped inside the imploding house of his nightmares,
Which the demons have again decided to dynamite.
But maybe this time the demolition will get done
In a matter of strategic ignitions from his synaptic wires,
So expeditiously and economically executed
By experts in explosives employed by his advanced age
That forgetting will arrive not as a disorienting surprise
But welcome admission into catatonia's domain,
That refuge where intellect and emotions
No longer hold sway
And vegetation is the conventional wisdom
Undertaken by inmates surviving in states of inanition,
Trying to complete their Ph.D.'s in lobotomy —
Half-wits, nitwits, idiots, Mad Hatters
Overcrowding the brain's insane asylum.

He awakens from barbed *Giftgas* hallucinations
Rising through dry-shower vents at Sobibor,
Perforating his desiccated pia mater
Like vibrating needles in the Penal Colony's contraption
Tattooing the twentieth century from forearm to arthritic wrist
With sadistic quadratic equations,
Whose blue numerals suggest inhuman applications:
Trials by baking, bullets, Zyklon B,
Innovative variations on a Grünewald dance of death,
Delusions of Aryan superiority, subterfuge, genocide . . .
Awakens into a sinister silence so shrill
His psyche's collapsing house deafens him;
His flesh turns to acrid plaster dust, his bones to rubble.
One day, some year, soon, now, never,
He'll be rescued or exhumed from this depression that buries him
Whenever he seeks sleep to escape night's sterile despair.

Turkey Truck

Caught behind a turkey truck
Roaring north on 63 toward Moberly,
Discouraged from passing
For the traffic heading into Columbia from the hinterlands,
He continues to cringe for the next thirty miles
As white feathers peel off,
Striking hood, windshield, his eyes
Like a December blizzard,

And all the while, those white phantoms,
Scraggly-plumed birds
Stuffed in boxes piled six high
Times perhaps twenty rows deep on each side,
Remain hypnotized
By their sixty-mile-an-hour ride.
Never do the feathers quit flying,
Though the snow changes to dandelion seeds briefly,

Then back to dirty feathers
As he finally closes the gap
To scrutinize victims in sinister cages,
Creatures forced to squat on stiff legs,
Unable to stand, stretch, switch positions,
Tiny, pink, lizardlike heads silent from fright,
Their ramshackle transport conveying his plucked spirit
Back to Dachau this gray day.

Tattoos

Even though the incident occurred last week,
Sitting in his cramped kitchen this Sunday morning,
He can vividly recall their brief conversation,
Graphically see that greenish-blue tattoo on her forearm,
Concealed beneath the wristband she brazenly lifted
After he inquired why she was wearing it,
Still feel himself shiver with surprise
Viewing that indelibly needled,
Sinister, spread-winged eagle
She claimed she'd acquired back in her native Germany
At least a decade ago,

She just one of a *Korps* of waitresses
Who service the Kaffee Haus, two blocks away,
Where, six days a week, he breakfasts,
Catches up on his newspaper-reading for an hour or three,
Depending on whim or fate's dictates,
Since he has no place to be, no dates to keep
With people who long ago left him alone
To baby-sit and lullaby the lifetime of stillborn memories
He miraculously resuscitated from the ashes of Auschwitz,
Belzec, Chelmno, Sobibor —
Every last, passive member of his massive family tree.

He could neither stop her nor desist from listening
As she told how, in love with a boy her own age
(He knew even now she must be only in her mid-twenties),
She'd had his initials permanently etched in her flesh,
A reckless, stupid gesture she soon came to realize,
After he jettisoned her for another girl.
Outraged, she'd returned to the parlor in Berlin
And requested something larger to hide those three letters,
Obliterate them forever beneath a more complex design,
An insignia with nationalistic overtones:
The two-headed eagle she held before his eyes.

Sitting at his kitchen table, sipping tea,
He twists his own left wrist ever so obliquely
To view that unevenly placed sequence of blue numerals
He's worn for more than forty years
And ponders the absurdity of history's inconsistency,
*

Which, by virtue of the diabolical irony of shared tattoos,
Would equate a Jewish survivor of the death camps
With a German youth sporting a crucifix on a gold necklace,
Reducing her, in his view, through a perversion of blood libel
Proscribed at Nuremberg as "crimes against humanity,"
To a Nazi perpetrator too.

Elusionist

Lately, sleep has been such an amorphous place,
An enigma whose conundrum
Is the only imaginable answer he can "put to bed,"
Tuck under his psyche's tattered sheets and comforter.
He just can't seem to find sleep easily anymore;
Its location is a barracks of starving,
Lice-ridden nightmares,
An entire *Lager* of chimerical hallucinations.
In fact, once naked each evening,
He feels bad dreams crawling all over his body,
Not so much like worms or baby snakes
But indelible tattoos on his sweaty flesh,
Whose proliferation of grotesque designs,
Composed of dangling eyes,
Severed heads, arms, breasts, and genitalia,
No artists have signed
Or affixed with their swastika remarques
To establish memory's official provenance.

Each morning, he arises inside a new husk,
Having painfully outgrown the old one
During the hours when his tossing and rolling
Might be that of his own calcified bones
Churning in a mixer, turning into cement
That lets him escape one self and fill tomorrow's mold,
Waiting at bed's edge to cast his next anonymous identity.
Who is he these days,
And what reason might he use to justify his survival?
These metaphysical questions are strictly physical;
There's no eluding their terrifying immediacy.
Suicide is not an option,
Despite the fact that cranial amniocentesis
Has clued him in to the truth:
He's doomed to live with his stillborn children,
Those disguises he assumes nightly
To prove that Auschwitz didn't neuter his spirit
Eternally.

Schlomo Vogelsang: Prague, Auschwitz, St. Louis

This steamy April a.m.,
Unusually humid for this season
Due to the torrential rain that poured all morning
On the roof of his brain,
He leaves the house drowsy,
Trips over the welcome mat,
Almost falls to the concrete
With both attachés beneath his spread-eagle feet,
But regains equilibrium
In time to focus on a budding tree,
From whose upper limbs echo the sweetest *Vogelsang*,
Perhaps the most beautifully fluid tunes
To which he ever remembers listening
With such mesmeric attention.

Suddenly, he realizes that the entire sky,
Spaces visible
As well as those which defy immediate vision,
Is itself a colossal aviary,
Filled not so much with tiny, precious, feathered bodies
As with notes, refrains, complete songs
Poetically flowing between similar species
Or at least not violating air zones
Belonging to disparate ones.
Everywhere, the air is ashimmer with twittering,
Chirping, cheeping, clucking, cooing,
Too many noises to hum or imitate
For their varying cadences and irregular pitches:
A hundred-piece orchestra tuning up.

Unable to move for what could be minutes,
Half an hour, decades,
He loses himself to spring's mellifluous music
Until bad dreams that burrowed through his sleep
Rise, like worms after deep rains,
To the surface of his waking spirit,
Divert him from his peaceful amnesia
To the business of getting to work precisely on time.
Making a strange leap, he conceives an idea:
*

Maybe he could feed his nightmares to the birds,
Who, in turn, might convert them into melodies
Capable of nourishing an earth
Just beginning to reflourish
And let him bequeath the universe his surname's legacy.

Destroying All Traces of Evidence

His amorphous shape awakens inordinately late
This spectral Wednesday morning.
He could be his own ghost groping for the location
Of its corporeal extermination
Or the soul of a spirit liquidated after its earthly ascent.
Either way, he's certain
That transubstantiation has abandoned him in a place
Where the air's only analogue is air,
Which he shares with vaporless shades combing space
For an opening out of the eternal maze.

A vague divination energizes his numb senses;
Brain waves pulsating despite decay
Alert his essence to enemies closing fast
From an unknown galaxy.
He dims the nimbus emanating from his nebula,
Hoping to avoid collision,
But destiny has his trajectory locked in.
Someone has informed the Gestapo of his diversionary tactics,
Exposed his Jewish heart below his convert's cross —
The SS has arrived to gather his ashes.

Yom Kippur for a Survivor

This dark, early Thursday a.m.,
There's fire in the sky,
An autumnal conflagration of disembodied spirits
Pulsating like northern lights
Reflecting across a lake's calm face,
A numinous cluster of depleted, incomplete souls
Orbiting their old home in a meteor shower,
Glowing particles that account for hued twilights,
Vermilion or hazy-pink dusks and dawns,
Depending on ice crystals and dust motes in the atmosphere,
Depending on parallaxes, angles of refraction,
Depending on willing suspensions of disbelief,
Depending on skepticism of science and religion,
Depending on the degree of forgiveness
Those who sacrificed their lives in the *Shoah*
Are willing to accord Elohim,

Since it's their celestial presences, their mandorlas,
Not His,
That cast a collective shadow at high noon,
Their raw, omniscient, unfinished mission
That promises first comings, eternal peace,
Not His,
Their ineffable vision of the ultimate infernal abyss
That he senses whenever, at Yom Kippur,
He asks God to repent,
Beg him for clemency from his final judgment of Him
For having abrogated His covenant,
Instead of beseeching Him
For dispensation from His Final Judgment of him.
This morning, his eyes cry tears of dry fire;
The Days of Awe, like Armageddon and Auschwitz,
Turn to *Kaddish*-flames, forgotten names, God-ashes.

Unscathed Refugees

Escaping Ghettos

For the last fifty years,
He's been funneling his fears
Into sewer tunnels of nightmares and daydreams,
Groping by candle-flicker like the Warsaw Jew he was,
Hoping against despair to disappear with them,
Burrow beneath intimidation's makeshift barriers
To freedom in a nearby Gorgon-forest,
Where escape is an illusion
In which only those uninitiated into the depths of solitude
Believe they can save themselves from shootings
By marauding *Einsatzgruppen*.
What amorphous anxieties these are
Even intuition can't fathom.
Oh, the torment he could have spared himself
If only a courageous few
Had revealed themselves to his watchful eye!

But by now in this late-life fugue,
With its Hollywood-backlot ghetto set,
He realizes his subterranean paranoia will never surface,
Despite hiding side by side with him.
His best chance is to jettison it, if possible,
Fend alone in old age's desolate unknown,
And trust that the enemy will never exhume fear's bones,
Exact graphic confessions of all the horrors he suffered
Before and after his descent
Into the seeping recesses of his unvented tunnel vision.
Perhaps he'll outlast his buried past,
Survive to ninety without once looking back
To that brief, peaceful season
When his two children, wife, and he,
Unaware they'd be forced underground,
Almost believed they belonged to the *Vaterland*.

Crow-Magnon Man

Although hardly original,
The act of awakening, this September a.m.,
Seems strange, surreal, disorienting,
As if his eyes were viewing a lunar landscape
Through a soaring horsefly's orbits
Or scanning a planet's densely cratered crust
With a space probe's telescope.
Even his naked body refuses to acknowledge him,
And his cold soul shows no signs
Of ever having operated his fleshly apparatus
Or infused his mind with life-passion.

In the intellect's galvanic zone,
Which memory energizes
Long after the spirit itself is pronounced brain dead,
He remains capable of resurrecting vocabulary
That superficially conveys his condition:
Anomie, ennui, invisibility —
Meursault's debilitating affectlessness,
K.'s and Gogo's nihilistic futility.
But these are just pseudo-psychobiographical,
Literarily therapeutic terms
That describe syndromes only fictive protagonists own.

This cool morning,
Portending winter in his bones,
Shivers with omens of loneliness.
Driving away from his temporary home,
He suffers an Old Testament locust-plague of crows
Crosshatching his vision not with outstretched talons
But wing tips flap-flapping their black bodies
Back and forth, from road to shoulder,
Their blurred motions not noticeably disturbed
By his approaching auto. As he passes,
He sees them pecking his flattened, bleeding carcass.

Daddies' Girls

An old sales rep who lost both daughters in the Holocaust,
He still cries silently
For those youthful Jewesses with whom he schmoozes
On business trips to college towns,
Who try to earn a "little extra change,"
Put themselves through school
By hostessing and waiting tables.
He's moved by the few who confide in him
That, despite unspoken restrictions and quotas,
They've entered golf and tennis tournaments,
For which their fathers have coached them,
At gentile country clubs.

He still cries inside, encountering them,
Those impetuous, well-educated daddies' girls,
Most of them away from home for the first time,
Eager to define their own identities,
Make a place for themselves in society,
Because he realizes that regardless of their talent,
Discipline, skill, and competitive spirit,
Fate has relegated these daughters of the Diaspora
To the Zyklon B showers
Even before they work up a sweat
Beating their vicious *shiksa* adversaries
At their own game — survival of the fittest.

He's witnessed them in his travels,
So intense, so self-confident,
So innocently determined to succeed
That they believe themselves exempt from foul play,
Rigged rounds, fixed matches,
As though centuries of oppression never existed.
Listening to them express their hopes and ambitions,
He squirms, wishing to admonish them somehow
That the referees are corrupt,
The line judges bigots, hypocrites, racists,
And that six-love and eight under par
Are always skewed in favor of privileged losers.

Oh, if only he could alert them to the truth,
That Jewesses, no matter how adroit,
How beautiful, how assimilative their dispositions,
Can't win and that winning is a sin
Punishable by "life" in concentration camps.
Tonight, dining alone, he double tips
His physically fit, Semitic-looking waitress,
Wishes her well with a silent *l'chaim*,
And prays she'll defeat each goy opponent
Who knocks on her door with vengeful challenges,
Knowing that whatever she does,
She'll always be death's whore.

The Best in the Business

Each restive night,
After spending another desperate day
Anxiously seeking a new hiding place
Where he might elude his mind's *Einsatzgruppen*,
Who've been hunting him down,
Noticeably gaining ground
(These days of his grand-mal-seizure malaise,
He can actually catch traces of their specters
Ransacking his rapid eye movements,
Ripping them to shreds
Trying to find his psyche's secret annex,
Which he appropriated from the Frank family in Amsterdam
When they were forced to vacate),
Combing all known coverts in his adopted towns
For those resourceful, misfortunate souls
Who escaped the swastika-scythe the first time around . . .

Each restively desperate cycle of twenty-four hours,
Dedicated to locating another Hooverville
In whose shabby purlieus he might sleep,
Under or, if he's lucky, between cardboard-box sheets,
Beneath a corrugated tin-roof or psychopathic sky,
Reduces his immune system by a few white cells,
Renders him slightly less capable of living by his wits.
After all, for over fifty years,
He's been engaged in this tricky business
Of making himself elusive to the Nazis,
Keeping in practice as a stunt man on movie crews,
Specializing in hanging from helicopters,
Falling off buildings, fighting underwater, skydiving,
Crashing motorcycles and cars,
Surviving mob squads and massive back-lot fires —
"Corky" Schwartz, escape artist par excellence.

Old Man Rosenblatt: Dresden, London, St. Louis

A man stands at the heart of an intersection
So spasmodic all its veins and arteries,
Merging at odd, dizzying angles,
Throb as if suffering a myocardial infarction;
Reds, yellows, and greens
Confuse each other with obscene pain
As though each were a clot signaling valves,
Not cars, to lock shut, stop,
Or, dissolving, go, flow through an open chute
Out of control — fate's chaos,
Which somehow avoids obeying its own fatal ukase.

At this swastika-like four-way junction,
He waits for the graphic that tells him to cross,
Patient despite the trafficked backwash
Spewing exhaust in his eyes,
Causing him to cry, choke,
Blow into a smudged handkerchief
He draws from a torn pocket
And wipes across his raw, dripping nose
To stanch the rusty flood.
Stunned, he notices blood instead of mucus
Running from somewhere deeper than his wells go.

Suddenly, he begins to shiver. In the distance,
A shrill pitch of sirens annihilates silence
His numb ears have become used to hearing
From having lived too many years
Too near the city's main highway,
A whine that grows into a low growl,
A groaning, bellowing moan,
As it approaches, exploding into a hydra,
Whose heads metamorphose into blurs
Nervously navigating constricted spaces
Made by autos willing themselves inconspicuous,

The blurs transforming into colossal fire trucks,
(Hook-and-ladder units, pumpers),
Police and emergency support vehicles,
Their crimson blips alternating maniacally,
*

Stippling storefronts, ladder rungs, fenders, and grilles.
His eyes fill with tears, go blind;
His throat tightens;
His nose won't quit bleeding.
He slumps to the sidewalk
And is lost amidst the pervasive disorder
That dominates this *danse macabre*.

Somewhere, tragedy fans itself into a fire,
Forcing this Dresden refugee of '38,
Who, before arriving in St. Louis, survived the London blitz,
To recall, all too vividly, the spitting cobra flames,
The 360-degree collapse of conflagrant buildings,
The claxons of ambulances and engines
Racing to pitiless obliterations and ash heaps,
Remember those horrific wails and screeches
Of V-2s shredding the shrouds of sky
Just long enough to find their assigned graves
In the blighted streets of Blighty —

This man, perfunctorily shuffling to the restaurant
Where he eats breakfast, lunch, and dinner daily,
Passing away from fright
In plain sight of a hundred inconvenienced souls,
Who, for ten or twenty seconds, have nodded off
Or played dumb to avoid personal involvement,
Dying unceremoniously, without anyone saying *Kaddish*
Or even so much as taking notice of his crumpled corpse
As they jam accelerators to floorboards —
Among them, only old man Rosenblatt
Late to his funeral today.

A Necessary Atavism

He awakens, this dreary, rain-blasted day,
With myriad wriggling nightmares
Clinging like bloated leeches to his wizened flesh.
He's sweating as though a spiking fever
Were driving him to the threshold of phantasmagoria,
Where he's a feather buffeted tumultuously in a tidal wave
On a waterless ocean shadowed by archaeopteryxes,
All of whom he suspects are his ancestors,
Each in an amazing state of preservation,
Whose eerie, open-air sepulcher beckons him near,
Sets up the most terrifying recognition he's ever experienced,
As if his existence as a solitary feather
Is all that remains of this prehistoric species of predator,
Whose bellicose psyche yet possesses him.

This antediluvian morning,
Death reverses his soul's vagrant trajectory.
He flies back to his disoriented self,
Converges on Earth's atmosphere from a vast, galactic distance,
And begins the arduous task of recreating the past
Gene by gene by gene,
Until the pieces of the ontological puzzle
Resurrect from miasmal mists and fossilized forgetting
Obscure visions of beasts wading, roaming, stalking, soaring,
Disturbing the terraqueous serenity with mortifying roars.
For the second time in creation, he witnesses his extinction;
Only, now, devolution absorbs him in its vortex:
He's man, barbarian, Neanderthal, saurian,
Archaeopteryx frantically ripping apart his entrails and heart.

A Curse on His Father's Successors

To this day, animosity fills his nostrils.
His ears still echo painfully
From the fear treachery instills
In those who must succumb to arrogant dictates
Made by scheming men
To reinforce misguided notions of grandeur and success.

How he ever escaped pre-Nazi Poland
With his genitalia intact,
Avoided capture at the merciless hands of administrators
Dedicated to Draconian force,
Goyaesque grotesquery, and the horrors of war
Waged in the name of free competition, he'll never know.

Even now, whenever he returns to Warsaw,
His nerves tauten;
His stomach knots in painful peristalsis;
His courage visibly falters
As he visits the office his father abdicated unwillingly
To a close associate, Herr Brutus . . .

Or was it Iago, Judas?
Memory forgets at some deeply seated psychic behest
Energized for his sole protection,
Yet time arrests his best intentions,
Sends him back to that season
When that blessed man was flung into the flames

By fate's arbitrary and impersonal determination.
To this very moment,
His father's visage arises out of that firestorm
Stippled with flying swastikas
The size of dying cows, henhouses, tires.
His silhouette, in profile,

Is a bloody, rusty razor
Cutting slivers off his myopic eyes.
Crying only underscores the horrible grief
His dad's mandated termination nurtures.
Each business trip he makes to this city
Renews recrimination and hatred.

This afternoon, he'll fly back to Paris,
Having made his appearance
Just long enough to affix his signature to documents
Without which the universe could not survive.
His brief obligation accomplished,
He spits backward, not waiting to hear the splatter.

Patriarch of the Seder

For "Aunt Lassie," Julius, and Joanie Frager,
in remembrance of blessed Joey

Despite his reputation as a tireless Job,
A regenerated scapegoat, all-forgiving,
He's still haunted by specters of Torquemada,
Third Reich apparitions ferreting *Juden*,
And arcane, anti-Semitic poets
Disguised as every generation's laureates.
He hides his anxiety well, bites his tongue
When he stares at the bright eyes and smiles
Of the children singing *"Had Gadyo."*

He cries beyond ranges his wife can perceive
In her most compassionate, intuitive penetrations
Of moody daydreams that descend on his face
Like stalactites in his cave of days.
He weeps in his sleep, squirms in his chair at work
As if he were burning in a Chelmno furnace,
Exuding putrid odors at a flaming stake
As medieval Madrileños gape,
Or being stoned in a pogrom stretching from Haman to Hitler.

Yet he still believes that God's eye
Lies at the moral core of the universe's Horeb
And that the most direct way to arrive there
Is by sitting at the head of the Seder table,
Recounting Yiddish fables,
Eating horseradish, parsley dipped in salt water
Without visibly gritting his gold teeth.
He toasts the sacramental fruit of the vine
By reciting the *Kiddush*'s lyrical *"Borei P'ri Ha-gafen."*

He keeps the mythic Mosaical covenant alive
By lighting candles, reading Scripture from the Torah
Every Friday night to an empty temple,
Refuses to violate Saturday's sacred Sabbath
Making business calls, eats kosher.
He decries Volkswagens and Leica cameras.
Once a year, he achieves consolation
From the children's excitement on opening the door
Through which Elijah may slip unnoticed,

And he fantasizes escaping, alongside the Prophet,
All the ethnic biases and xenophobias
Bigots have loaded unmercifully on the feeble years.
He dreams of outracing the trains
And blowing up their tracks, dismantling Herr Krupp
One precise breech and muzzle at a time.
Only, a real hero he'll never be,
Rather patriarch of the Seder, filled with guilt for,
And cosmic fear from, his unassailed abundance.

Feinstein the Clothier

Heading to breakfast early,
Coursing down streets desolate and wet,
As though he's been preceded by a medieval plague,
He ponders his alienation,
The isolation he's endured for decades,
Since fleeing Berlin in November of '38.

This changeless town changes daily
His basic attitude toward dying and death.
Both he and it are twin insects,
Blending into themselves and the environment
That supports their symbiotic natures;
Each conceals the other from the enemy, life.

Stasis is sovereign, whose reciprocal ukase
Demands of its minions compromise,
Equivocation, greed. Neglect and denial,
Rather than impeding competition,
Speed up the process,
Risk being cited for conflict of interest

As faction pits itself against cabal
To restrain pornography, adultery,
Controlled substances, door-to-door solicitation,
Movements of Polacks, fags, Gypsies, niggers, and kikes.
They bonfire books with Hitlerian zeal,
Jam radio and television waves,

Lobby against new industry —
Progress in any form — from deep suspicions
That something might give,
Destroy the "quality of life" they've enjoyed
Since before century's turn.
They teach their children faith in Jesus,

Convinced that the greatest good
Can only be gleaned, literally, chapter and verse,
A line, a word at a time, from Christian Scripture.
As he nears Franck's Café,
Parks his car, and approaches,
A stark shiver whispers his bones to a high pitch.

His beaked nose and other Hebraic features betray him.
His face heats up,
Burns his forced smile to a tight scar.
No matter how he tries
To evade the regulars' penetrating eyes,
His thoughts are impaled, and fears speared.

Suddenly, he's a voyeur,
Peeking through these Peeping Toms' keyhole.
Neither criminal nor victim exactly,
He shrivels into a convenient booth
To listen to their impugning conversations,
Waiting for inevitable allusions to his Judaism.

Soon, he'll leave, throw open the doors
To his Factory Outlet Emporium,
Attend, with feigned enthusiasm, their wives' bovine wiles,
Solicitously help fit these town fathers
Into flawed bargains as well,
Momentarily forget what they said at breakfast,

And lose sight of his second-class position
In the town's great pecking order of being.
Once selling gowns, girdles, bras, blouses, and skirts,
Boxers, blazers, ties, tube socks, and boots,
He'll suppress slurs he heard earlier;
Depressing cash-register keys

Will anesthetize him to his dislocation.
But for now, his bony fingers
Caress the chipped china coffee cup
As if it were a chalice from which Moses sipped
Or the Grail filling with Christ's dripping blood.
He focuses on the courthouse across the street,

Watching ubiquitous pigeons hover and scurry
In a flurry of loose feathers and blurred hues.
He can almost see out through their eyes,
Hear their idiotic murmurs issuing from his throat,
Feel their shit evacuating his tract,
Splattering on the town's sacrosanct marble steps.

Scarecrow on a Crucifix

He, a fleshly scarecrow
Dressed in naked tatters to scatter rapacious crows
And other predators within the vicinity,
Steps out this frigid, late-September morning
And shivers from head to toe.
His bones clatter like aluminum cans
Rattling in a croker sack a bum swags over his shoulder
Or stones of a desecrated synagogue
Falling to the streets surrounding it
After birds and squirrels have ravaged its mortar
Until, like Gaudí's Iglesia di Sagrada Familia,
Only the facade exists —
Maybe our Architect
Never intended to finish our interiors,
Purposely meant for us to exist incomplete.

As his spectral flesh flaps in the bracing air,
He slaps his cheeks, rubs his fingers on stubble
He forgets to shave for days on end,
Just to confirm his appearance conforms to human features.
His shadow is a shabby apparition
Slicing through the sun's ravenous glare.
Staring into a rain puddle,
His eyes don't recognize his reflection or care to investigate
The similarity between the being they register
And the golem he's become,
Whose loose straw the crows will carry off all afternoon,
Cawing ferociously as they shred his crucified spirit,
Transmogrify it piecemeal in their beaks,
Until they've reduced him to the field he's been assigned —
This ghettoed Golgotha.

Children of a
Stillborn Generation

Why Didn't My Father Die in the Fire?

Sometimes I wish my dad had died at Auschwitz,
So that all my fantasized anguish
Could have a basis in history's stacks —
Not musty libraries' but crematories' —
By having risen with his soul from Topf and Sons ovens,
So that my morbid paranoia
Wouldn't sizzle and crisp my naked brain
With such relentless torment
Each time I read another grotesque account of the Holocaust
Or focus on incriminating images of genocide
Committed in the high cause of Hitler's spiritual vision
To rid first the world,
Then the entire universe, of Jew-vermin
With what, after many sloppy attempts with *dushegubki*
And Babi Yar and Ponar ravines and forests,
He finally discovered to be the most expeditious means
Ever devised by the human intellect
To systematically obliterate hundreds at a time:
Giftgas — that ghastly Teutonic insecticide.

Why couldn't my eighty-four-year-old father,
Whom I so admire for his moral fiber and right reason,
His tenacity, fairness, and perspicacity in business,
His compassion toward those less successful,
Have died in that European scourge,
When he would have been at his strength's peak,
Just as many of his peasant relatives from Kiev
And other desolations deep in the Ukraine,
Who, for destiny's sleight of hand,
He never even knew existed,
Had all their genealogical stocks and bonds
Placed in Hitler's blind-trust fund
And watched them go up in flames?
Why couldn't he too have died in the *Shoah*,
So that April 17, 1941,
Never would have liberated me from nonexistence,
Instead spared me having to waste my days
Grieving for all those ashen ghosts
Of my gassed and cremated heritage?

The Master Gardeners

Was it apathy or fear
That nourished the seeds in the Warsaw garden
Hans Frank tended?
Who could have dreamed
They would assume such motley blossoms,
Carmine and rust, suspended in nude humiliation
On tulip-slender stalks
Before the scythe cut across the entire plot
Like a shadow cast earthward from a V-2 rocket?

Why weren't the beautiful, supine flowers
At least allowed to mature,
So they could be sold from booths on Munich streets
Into aesthetic servitude
As useless decorations in the cut-glass universe
Of Prussian stuffiness
Instead of being snapped at the spine by shrapnel
Or systematically sprayed for lice
With Zyklon B pesticide?

By degrees, tenacious and extravagant ivy
Grew up above healed crevasses
Loaded with the severed stems and petals.
In later years,
Scientists coming to the greenhouses at Auschwitz,
Treblinka, Belzec, Chelmno, Majdanek, and Sobibor
Could only speculate
As to what fertilizers might have been used
To produce so furious and unexpungeable a bloom.

Ultimate Sacrifices

Yesterday was Ash Wednesday.
I could tell something was in the air besides spring,
With its crocuses, jonquils,
And forsythias sporadically blossoming,
Could see the difference immediately in the Kaffee Haus,
Where, mornings ad infinitum,
The businessmen of St. Louis's affluent West County
Congregate to map out their stratagems
For acquiring the entire kingdom
By their own "imminent"-domain chicaneries;
It was crowded with boisterous kids out of uniform,
Off from their local parochial schools
To observe the first day of Lent,
Marking Easter's arrival about forty days away.

Strange how the mind sometimes needs space
To assimilate stimuli. In my case,
It wasn't until late yesterday afternoon,
When I asked an old friend, a practicing Catholic,
To explain the meaning of Lent
And listened to him orate:
"Oh, you know. It has to do with mortality,
Ashes to ashes, dust to dust."
I remained silent while my pal pontificated,
"*You* know what ashes symbolize — Auschwitz, Dachau.
For *us*, it's a season of atonement,
The beginning of a process ending with Easter,
Our time for sacrificing and starting over,
As Christ died, was buried, and rose again for us."

This morning, just one day later,
I break fast with toast and coffee
And reflect on things my buddy said,
Especially how he'd vowed to give up extramarital sex —
For the next three fortnights.
The café is back to its normal capacity
For shenanigan-manufacturing and double-dealing.
I feel secure amidst all this duplicity,
Certain, at least, that nothing unpredictable,
Like a gang of schoolchildren off for a holiday,
*

Will disturb my ritual.
I come here daily to take Jewish communion,
No matter Ash Wednesday or Yom Kippur,
Remember those of the *Shoah*, who rose for no one.

An Incantatory Chant

On my own out here
This blindingly bright morning in the something of May,
Some year, some century, some millennium,
Gyved to a gaseous, red-hot rock
Flaming like a sun belching at the center of a system
Lost in the inner space of the outermost galaxy
In a universe not yet invented by God,
My wrists and ankles squeezed numb by goatskin bindings
Shriveling under the intense heat,
Rock and writhing body
Synonymous with the River Phlegethon's chaos,
I scream through the pain of burning alive
Inside my hallucinatory silence.

No echoes or responsive oracles testify to my presence;
Only the sounds of flesh hissing, crackling,
And bones exploding under the pressure
Of subliming superheated vapors
Set up a dialogue between *nihil* and psyche,
Remind me that my dislocation suits my anonymity.
I may be an unidentified flying object
Or test-tube spore efflorescing into a viral nightmare —
Ebola, anthrax, an apocalyptic strain unnamed as yet,
Capable of devastating a planet's entire population
Just by escaping its glass vial for five seconds
Before some dazed night watchman
Can restopple it with his finger
And replace it on the table
From which he's accidentally knocked it;
I might be a rotting carcass of crow or tyrannosaur
Hanging by its talons or clawed toes,
Naked as upside-down Mussolini,
From a Piranesian meat hook
Suspended from the eye of a cosmic needle
Stitching the ripped seam in Joseph's many-colored robe,
That Biblical raiment handed down from generations
Of Angles, Saxons, Jutes, Huns, and Franks,
Ostrogoths and Visigoths,
Through the learned doctor of all 19th-century enlightenment,
Herr Professor Diogenes Teufelsdröckh of Weissnichtwo,
*

To those geniuses of zealotry and random vandalism
And absolute, fanatical worship of racial purification,
Who assumed names that rattled and screeched
Like a wagon train of empty aspirations
Heading westerly over a mud-rutted, rock-clotted road,
Groping for a cut in the Great Divide
Separating death and life,
Where they might hide throughout eternity
From their heinous crimes against humanity,
Perpetrated in the name of their own brand of demonology,
NAZISM,
Names whose very syllables, lethal as AIDS,
Fed fires of the plague
That would eventually consume them in its virulence,
Syllables that begat even more evil phonemes,
Begetting vocables whose trials by ordeal
Became the standards and calling cards
Of a fabled race of barbarians
Whose heroes, saints, martyrs
Would ultimately enter Valhalla's sacred precincts
By its basement door, *Hölle*,
Before being officially installed by the grand wizard,
Satan,
Names ghastly, plangent, shrill as V-2s spiraling down,
Names whose spoken detonations obliterate reason,
Names recognizable by their snorts, roars,
Growls, howls, caws, caterwauling loon calls,
Names that reek of bubbling human fat,
Splattering grease of eyes, tongues, breasts, penises,
Testicles, lungs, brains, kidneys, livers,
Intestines, bladders, prostates,
Names more acrid than singeing hair and nails,
Names crying out to return to infancy,
Before they became infected with the dread disease hubris,
Names scientists reserve for terminal cancers,
Names who, in naming their names,
Commit suicide in the name of genocidal shame and guilt,
Names so deep you can drop them into themselves
And never hear them hit bottom:
*

Doenitz, Ribbentrop, Hess,
Heydrich, Himmler, Göring, Goebbels, Bormann,
Jodl, Speer, Eichmann, Mengele,
Hitler,
That blasphemous litany of jarring, raucous aberrations
Reaching crescendo in the maniacal logorrhea of one man,
One absurdly mustachioed evangelist
Preaching nationalism, militarism,
And the glorification of an Aryan people of the north,
Who descended from tribal hordes,
Deracinating the Roman Empire,
Dethroning their gods, replacing them with Odin and Thor,
Substituting superstition for law,
Forcing the accused to engage in Teutonic witch hunts
By dunking their arms in boiling water
Or having them pick up white-hot iron bars
To prove their innocence — if, in three days,
Their burns were healed, they were set free; if not, hanged —
Eschewing the Roman stone roads,
Eschewing trade with neighboring cities and nations,
Abandoning the use of money, the need for communication,
Abandoning towns, trade, industry,
Resorting to farming as the sole means of sustenance,
Ownership of the land devolving to lords ruling manors,
Great estates owing allegiance to themselves,
Not to the peasants,
Abandoning education and cultural activities,
Abandoning ancient literature,
Architecture, sculpture, painting,
Supplanting Greek and Roman wisdom
With book-burning ignorance,
Entering the cave of dark ages,
From which they would emerge tentatively in 1871,
Then again in 1933,
Only to descend once more, in 1945,
Into the roaring furnaces and rubble of final judgment,
But not before taking with them in ignominious rout
Millions of innocent souls,
Seeds cast adrift,
*

Growing as ash-flowers in heavenly gardens
Somewhere beyond comprehension,
Beyond rational fathoming,
Beyond decent burial,
Beyond memorialization in Holocaust museums
Proliferating faster than concentration camps once did,
Which serve as living reminders
Of the uselessness, humiliation, and degradation
Of dying without due process,
Without being judged by a jury of peers,
Without being allowed to abide by the laws of the land
Beyond the land where the *Reichskanzler* resided
Inside his not-so-secret Berghof above Berchtesgaden,
Not far below his Eagle's Nest retreat,
Not quite crowning the Kehlstein in the Bavarian Alps,
Beyond this blindingly bright morning in the something of May,
Some year, some century, some millennium
So distant from past and future

That all I can do is try to fantasize my personal freedom,
Imagine myself biting loose from the goatskin shackles
That gyve me to hallucination's red-hot rock,
So that in one unfelling swoop
I might disassemble memory
And think myself clear to a defensible reason
Why I should continue waking each day,
Continue believing that faith is salutary
And that change will ameliorate man's shabby condition,
Continue, today, trusting yesterday's enemies,
Continue listening to my own heart
Whispering in cadences only the wind can translate
And the stars hear this far away from Nowhere,
Praying the possibility exists
That on another shore light-years beyond Forever,
Some spirit just might be receiving my SOS,
Some agent, force, invention
Able to transmit a signal that will reach me before I die,
A divination assuring me
That mercy and peace are yet worshiped elsewhere.

Paranoia for Breakfast

It's a matter of conditioning, nationalistic pride,
A collective genetic defect, egotistical brain damage,
That penchant for and preoccupation with gratuitous cruelty,
Malevolence in the abstract and as black fact
We creatures of the species *Homo sapiens* demonstrate daily.
First and last causes pale in light of original sin;
Original sin gives way to survival of the fittest.
Perhaps it all emanates from human nature's failure
To appreciate its own fragile ties with life,
Discriminate between ignorance and intellect,
Daydreams and nightmares, means and ends.
And maybe not.

When I contemplate man's myriad extirpations —
Individual homicides, tribal massacres,
Genocides decimating hundreds of thousands at a crack —
Groping to explain the common denominator, hatred,
I get tangled in a fence of Medusa-snakes
Disguised as righteous motives,
Lacerate my face on the fallacious blood-libel barbs
Perpetuated by history's pariahs: Pharaohs, *Führer*s,
Duces, Popes, pretenders to thrones,
Zealots, and terrorists fulfilling holy missions —
Sadistic, sociopsychopathic fanatics all.
No rational answer clarifies the operative "why."

This morning, sipping coffee in a packed café,
I almost flagellate myself publicly
For dwelling on such an irreconcilable subject.
Disgust stultifies my desire to drive to the library,
Dig through the ruins of books,
Hoping to retrieve relics of mankind's creeds,
Redemptive deeds done in the name of faith, compassion, love.
There's no justifying my foolish delusion,
And now, the noisy voices in this restaurant
Are crows cawing, clawing my skull, maggots gnawing my guts,
Death's aggressive advocates
Discussing the most expeditious way to dispose of my bones.

Schindlerjuden

For Thomas Keneally

Yesterday, having arrived one hour early
For the 4 p.m. showing of *Schindler's List*,
Standing near the head of a rapidly extending line,
I scanned the faces of accumulating strangers
Patiently keeping their places,
Not bunching up, shoving, but not giving ground,
Jewish faces almost exclusively, like mine,
Waiting to be told to submit our tickets,
Proceed down the corridor, to the fourth door,
Assume spaces from which we'd watch
Our own potential futures pass in review,
As though they, it — destiny — were a Pathé newsreel
Reprising a normal *Judenrein*-day in Poland or Germany
From 1941 through April 1945 . . .

The ceaseless waiting grating on us,
Growing more enervating, until, en masse, we perked up,
Alert to phantoms, ghosts, poltergeists,
Dazed souls exiting through a narrow passage,
Those who'd just seen what we were about to witness —
Oh, those drawn, grim, gaunt, chalky faces,
So forlorn, morose, etched with inarticulate grief,
Their liberated spirits empty of tears, fear-ridden,
Groping to locate themselves in the hysterical mall
As though it were more than a matter of eyes
Accommodating to the bright lights
After all that black-and-white subjugation of the senses,
Trying to distinguish that haven from the eerie desolation
At whose depot gates they had just been jettisoned,

Corralled by what sinister manner of beast
Or sadistic executioner of crimes in the name of the Reich
None could begin to conceive . . . that crowd so somber
They might have made up a funeral procession
Or been the walking dead, possessed by mind-parasites.
Now, a day later, I no longer rely on memory
So much as intuition to lead me to these conclusions:
Yesterday might as easily have been Auschwitz,
Not a theater, and I one of thousands
*

Led to the Zyklon B gassing showers
Or to Topf and Sons ovens,
Finally floating, sifting, spiraling inside the vast draft,
Up through that immense, roaring chimney stack
Spewing millions of tons of European Jew-ash into oblivion,

Instead of just another moviegoer
Surrendering to the magic of a Sunday matinée,
Watching a critically acclaimed recreation of the Holocaust
As seen through the eyes of one German-Catholic Nazi,
Oskar Schindler,
Who somehow made that mystical leap
From crass Teutonic capitalist
To righteous angel
Inscrutably moved away from greed and base venality,
Toward that rarefied selflessness
Only a few saints and fewer apostles have ever known,
In which saving one human being saves humanity;
Ironically, God gave him the power to whisper *Kaddish*
Over his own Aryan bones as well.

Finally, back in the insulated womb of my writing office
(Not unlike Don Quixote's broom closet,
Where I hide from dawn to dusk daily,
Writing poems I deludedly believe will make a difference
In a world cursed with bigotry and violence,
A difference capable of affecting someone,
Anyone who reads my pleas for peace, mercy,
Giving as the only true means of receiving),
I realize what drew me to that theater yesterday afternoon
And caused me to hallucinate so graphically:
An unslakable need to belong to that group of people,
Living and long gone,
Whose song, no matter how lugubrious,
Derives its ancient invocation, *Shema, Yisrael*, from God's lips.

Setting Santayana on the Back Burner

Those who cannot remember the past
are condemned to repeat it.
— George Santayana

Beasts of all species
Show their truest colors
When strangling their mates
By degrees of passion and hatred
Leading to plangent genocide.
Like a pulsating penis
Penetrating an albino cobra,
My pen ejaculates semen
With the odor of smoldering flesh,
That black, acrid disdain
Racism has for its enemies.
My brain's outraged senses
Flop like Moby Dick
On the deck of the cosmic *Rachel*,
Roaming the oceans alone
In search of its lost children,
Satanic Hitler's orphans,
Burned in the drought of ages,
Hoping to find their reflections,
Disguised as fugitive clouds,
Undulating in the waves,
Floating below the surface
As gracefully as dolphins and porpoises,
Schools of beautiful memories.
But my words turn from sperm to semen
To water leaking from my pen,
Then to crystal-clear tears
Dripping to my paper, splattering,
Smearing the red ink,
Swirling my images to blood,
Blood to disgust to repugnance.

Suddenly, I see myself
Whirling in a tornado's vortex
Rising up from the page,
A wind devil spouting a halo,
An eerie, crimson mandorla,
*

The spirit of those who died
Rising into the angry sky
To claw its eyes blind,
Rip its hide from its body,
Set fire to its carcass,
That its ashes might evaporate
In the vast, airless Nowhere,
The soul's *Hölle*,
To which go the earth's psychopaths,
Murderers with massive appetites,
After the last battles are fought
And lost to the victims' issue
Who survive by proxy or default
To tell their cautionary axiom,
That forgetting disasters of the past
Or refusing to heed its misdeeds
Dooms them to future lunacies,
Bestial catastrophes.

Springtime of a Neo-Nazi

Spring is any hour,
Any day, any decade now,
Or so he's been told by the Gestapo
Occupying his most indignantly cynical senses,
Those organs of his fancy
Milton subverted through his chameleonic Prince of Lies,
The Chief of Propaganda, Lucifer Goebbels,
Architect of his mind's Fourth Reich,
Whose sole duty is to drill fresh seeds of evil design
That will flower profusely into even more vile deeds
Done in the obscene name of the "Holohoax."

Just imagine how one fine April morning
He'll gaze from his Berchtesgaden rooftop
And see Alpine valleys
Overflowing with *fleurs du mal*–swastikas
Swaying down mountainsides,
Disguised as *Luftwaffe*-blossoms,
Damned panzer-plants,
Storm-trooper doom-blooms.
How beautiful that view of renewed abundance!
He'll need at least a hundred million people to sow
And a millennium or two to reap all the harvests.

Defacing Gravestones

Who ever knew such bucolic seclusion as I do,
This lush, lonely evening,
Seated outdoors amidst such supple greenery?

Yet who ever conceived being alone
Could be so unreciprocated that even bushes and trees,
Spireas, lilacs, magnolias, mimosas, oaks,

Would refuse to acknowledge my fragile presence at this table?
I am just me, Lord,
Trying to see, beyond this paltry moment's emptiness, eternity,

Glimpse that paradisiacal rim,
At which point peaceful coexistence among men
Assumes the dignity of docile robins, gentle wrens.

Out here, away from all my wayward enemies
And very occasional friends,
My gray matter contemplates eschatological options.

Listening to nature's creatures
(Cicadas, birds and squirrels, crickets and bats),
I remember the origin of my own bones:

They are of those fated generations of chosen Jews
Dr. Mengele tried to clone in his labs
To learn how to create a superior race of Aryans.

But if he succeeded, how, then, can I be sitting here,
Decades later, scribbling fragments of nightmares
I've not experienced, only imagined?

Why, amidst such bucolic seclusion,
Am I compelled to search these recesses
For essences, odors, ghostly reminiscences?

Is it that I distrust silence
And keep constant vigil against possible invasion
By invisible foes? Who are they?

Seated outside, seventy-five miles from St. Louis,
In this town not only time but the Bible forgot,
I'm not precisely certain where or who my being is.

Suffice it for me to record that on this quiet June night,
When no humans dare intrude on my writing,
I have spent the better part of twilight's illumination

Composing my doubts, tuning those few ideas
That years of practice have enabled me to express,
Formulating metaphors I might use in a pinch

To help me deduce the reason for my very existence.
Right now, listening to birds, crickets, squirrels, locusts,
Balancing the moon on the focal point of my eyes,

I die ten thousand times each second,
Seduced by the ecstasy that enraptures me in its voices,
Sounding noises I can see and sense and smell.

I can't escape this extrasensory, oxymoronic Heaven/Hell;
It's as though Auschwitz-Birkenau-Buna
Has relegated me to its precincts, adopted me as its scapegoat.

Out here, amidst all this teeming loudness, I expire.
Slowly, the gonads surrender.
Within hours, my fleshly vessel lists, sinks;

No holds are barred; no zones remain sacred.
The misfit I've become resigns himself to watching fireflies
Scorch the empty spaces with their radical ignitions.

As darkness descends, quashing all traces of light,
Night retires to its caves,
While I hysterically seek shelter

Within the folds of my own cerebral cortex.
Reflexes slow; the testicles clot.
I retreat, as though Satan has ordered me

To repeat civilization's ancient mistake.
Now, only the full moon remains
To guide me home to my bed.

By default, I agree to accept her questionable advice.
(Wisdom is not even in the running — not even!)
Soon, too soon, I find myself between sheets,

A sad, baffled, complacent human being
Not altogether unwilling to accept defeat on its terms
Or averse to listening to Berchtesgaden treaties

Not hitherto rehearsed by Austrian revolutionaries
Who sign their paintings "Adolf"
And goose-step every chance they get.

Tonight, I'm willing to die without regret
Or continue living despite myself;
Whichever design God chooses is fine by me.

I'm resigned to His decision, resigned to mine.
By tomorrow, I'll not even recognize the face,
Texture of the flesh, the mind that motivated me

To write such tripe on night's gravestone:
Here lies the jettisoned essence of a diaspora poet
Who died a lifetime ago.

Obscene Echoes

Heading to the local restaurant for breakfast,
I enter Monday morning's cold November drizzle,
Arch my back, bare my teeth, and growl
As though my riled canine psyche
Could intimidate all demons still aborting memory.
Once seated in my usual booth,
I contemplate the start of another workweek,
Weaving strategies to outwit the Sphinx,
Minotaur, and Rudolf Hess,
Escape between pyramids, from Labyrinths,
And avoid xenophobic, ghettoing rhetoric
Chelmno mentalities express,
Hellbent on cleansing their race
Of virulent, non-Teutonic strains
By raising hatred to a Fourth Reich power of violence
Even too frightening to have emanated from Satan's crew.
These grisly, spectral premonitions are today's Germany,
The reunified virus,
Not the phage from the '30s and '40s
But the '90s swastika version of bigotry,
Perpetuated by neo-Nazi adults not too old to forget
And skinheads young enough to reinvent the nightmare's wheel
From sheer ignorance and belligerent anomie.

Why, safely insulated in Schatzenkamer's Bavarian Inn,
Located in the very heart of America's Midwest,
I'm assailed by these harpy-faced effigies of the Holocaust
Has less to do with this place's Germanic motif
(Steins, coats of arms, paintings of castles on the Rhine)
Than with *USA Today*'s front-page photo
Crowded with bald teenagers shouting silent obscenities
My ears can hear all this distance from Tübingen,
Heidelberg, Düsseldorf, Berlin.

Herr Clement of Buenos Aires

You scrawny, gaunt, arrogant bastard!
How dare you flaunt your Aryan polemics
In cold, bold austerity,
Blindfolded, at the end of your taut-drawn rope,
Caught finally in a cul-de-sac
Of a labyrinth fifteen years intricate.

Just a cog in a colossal gear train, you reiterate.
And it was your doing
That brought about subtle changes
In the carrying out of the Final Solution:
A chocolate for the children before the showers
So they wouldn't fear

What their peristaltic stomachs,
Spastic valves, and hammering hearts
Had already made them privy to
Out of the ancient, miasmic oppression;
A Strauss waltz, improvised by prisoners
Not yet metamorphosed by the Zyklon B alembic

Into more blackened bones for the smoldering,
To ease the older ones into oblivion —
This was also your contribution to mankind.
How considerate, Herr Monster,
To wear a skin graft in the armpit,
Where your SS number once pulsed!

How perfectly sensitive of you, Herr Satan,
Who said when you die
You'd leap into your grave,
Taking six million Jews with you!
Well, now the time has finally arrived
To let your prophecy fulfill itself.

Trial is too good,
Because it's righteous and moral.
Any schoolkid knows you can't add apples and goats,
Let alone crossbreed different species.
Races . . . ah, yes! They can be exterminated,
Hybridized through stirpiculture;

Even Mendel wouldn't deny the possibilities.
But adjudication of madness is delusion,
Madness of another kind.
Yet we bring you to trial, Herr Eichmann,
For crimes against humanity, genocide.
Even though we realize the absurdity

Of thinking in terms of reprisals, reparations,
Your execution is far too lenient.
Neither the total effacement of your indignation
Nor your signed confession of guilt can assuage the dead,
Who live in Canaan, near the Mediterranean,
Into which we'll cast your ashes.

Ishmael Fishman

What manner of obscene beasts are these horrific nightmares
That have forced me to breach sleep's burning surface,
Beach on day's shore
Before being transported to nearby Sobibor
Or, if sidetracked by chaos,
Shipped farther down and out the line,
To Chelmno, Auschwitz, Belzec, Treblinka, or Majdanek?
Are they "chosen" Kapos or purebred Nazis,
Inculcated with Satan's hissing viciousness and disdain
For *Untermenschen* and other fated human beings
Slated for Operation Reinhard's *Endlösung*?
Or is it conceivable I've just imagined myself dead
For lesser reasons than wanting to be
The living answer to the Jewish Question,
A black sacrificial lamb
Existing yet amidst a pack of Teutonic wolves
Dressed in sheep's jackboots and bleached-fleece uniforms?

Could it be that imagination has, once more,
Gotten the better of my mind by playing charades,
Relying on my identification
With history's litany of Holocaust atrocities —
By now almost stock metaphors for "man's inhumanity to man,"
Itself a Burnsian cliché —
To persuade me that my victimization
Owes its propagation not to my creative capacity
But to actual events from half a century ago?
I'd like to believe my torment
Has its origins in others' misfortune,
But the truth is, I can only blame my masochistic self
For reinventing my gruesome tale:
I'm the Jew-poet called Ishmael,
Adrift on an oceanic boneyard of pogroms,
Still hoping to arrive home safe, somewhere,
With an answer to the riddle of the leviathan's whiteness.

Epilogue

The Bitter Riddles of History

For Elie Wiesel

Why does memory forget itself so easily?
Why do successive generations let grief and regret fade,
Until all that's left are those old demons —
Xenophobia, hostility, anti-Semitism —
And the fear of being invaded,
Violated, and exterminated by supermen
Bent on racial purification, ethnic cleansing,
And the next decades' euphemisms for genocide?

Why are history's bitter riddles so mystifying,
Cryptic, inextricably mixed
With the DNA of culture's collective conscience?
When will man decipher the ancient codes
To elitism, egotism, and societal violence,
Those intervening variables that never vary?
How is forgetting like a vampire?
Who or what will thrust a Star of David through its heart?

Biographical Note

Louis Daniel Brodsky was born in St. Louis, Missouri, in 1941, where he attended St. Louis Country Day School. After earning a B.A., magna cum laude, at Yale University in 1963, he received an M.A. in English from Washington University in 1967 and an M.A. in Creative Writing from San Francisco State University the following year.

From 1968 to 1987, while continuing to write poetry, he assisted in managing a 350-person men's clothing factory in Farmington, Missouri, and started one of the Midwest's first factory-outlet apparel chains. From 1980 to 1991, he taught English and creative writing at Mineral Area Junior College, in nearby Flat River. Since 1987, he has lived in St. Louis and devoted himself full-time to composing poems. He has a daughter and a son.

Brodsky is the author of thirty-six volumes of poetry, five of which have been published in French by Éditions Gallimard. His poems have appeared in *Harper's*, *Southern Review*, *Texas Quarterly*, *National Forum*, *Ariel*, *American Scholar*, *Kansas Quarterly*, Ball State University's *Forum*, *New Welsh Review*, *Cimarron Review*, *Orbis*, and *Literary Review*, as well as in five editions of the *Anthology of Magazine Verse and Yearbook of American Poetry*.

Also available from **Time Being Books**

EDWARD BOCCIA
No Matter How Good the Light Is: Poems by a Painter

LOUIS DANIEL BRODSKY
You Can't Go Back, Exactly
The Thorough Earth
Four and Twenty Blackbirds Soaring
Mississippi Vistas: Volume One of *A Mississippi Trilogy*
Falling from Heaven: Holocaust Poems of a Jew and a Gentile
  (with William Heyen)
Forever, for Now: Poems for a Later Love
Mistress Mississippi: Volume Three of *A Mississippi Trilogy*
A Gleam in the Eye: Poems for a First Baby
Gestapo Crows: Holocaust Poems
The Capital Café: Poems of Redneck, U.S.A.
Disappearing in Mississippi Latitudes: Volume Two of *A Mississippi Trilogy*
Paper-Whites for Lady Jane: Poems of a Midlife Love Affair
The Complete Poems of Louis Daniel Brodsky: Volume One, 1963–1967
Three Early Books of Poems by Louis Daniel Brodsky, 1967–1969: *The Easy
  Philosopher*, *"A Hard Coming of It" and Other Poems*, and *The Foul Rag-
  and-Bone Shop*

HARRY JAMES CARGAS (editor)
Telling the Tale: A Tribute to Elie Wiesel on the Occasion of His 65th
  Birthday — Essays, Reflections, and Poems

JUDITH CHALMER
Out of History's Junk Jar: Poems of a Mixed Inheritance

GERALD EARLY
How the War in the Streets Is Won: Poems on the Quest of Love and Faith

ALBERT GOLDBARTH
A Lineage of Ragpickers, Songpluckers, Elegiasts & Jewelers: Selected
  Poems of Jewish Family Life, 1973–1995

ROBERT HAMBLIN
From the Ground Up: Poems of One Southerner's Passage to Adulthood